SEED, SPROUT, FRUIT

An Apple Tree Life Cycle

BY SHANNON KNUDSEN

ILLUSTRATED BY SIMON SMITH

Consultant: Allison Parker, MS, RD
Director, Consumer Health and Education
U.S. Apple Association

CAPSTONE PRESS
a capstone imprint

First Graphics are published by Capstone Press,
1710 Roe Crest Drive, North Mankato, Minnesota 56003.
www.capstonepub.com

Library of Congress Cataloging-in-Publication Data

Knudsen, Shannon, 1971–
  Seed, sprout, fruit : an apple tree life cycle / by Shannon Knudsen; illustrated by
Simon Smith.
      p. cm.—(First graphics. Nature cycles)
  Summary: "In graphic novel format, text and illustrations describe the life cycle of
an apple tree"—Provided by publisher.
  Includes bibliographical references and index.
  ISBN 978-1-4296-5366-4 (library binding)
  ISBN 978-1-4296-6230-7 (paperback)
  1. Apples—Juvenile literature. I. Title. II. Series: First graphics. Nature cycles.
  SB363.K68 2011
  634'.11—dc22   2010029084

Editor: **Gillia Olson**
Designer: **Lori Bye**
Art Director: **Nathan Gassman**
Production Specialist: **Eric Manske**

Printed in the United States of America in Eau Claire, Wisconsin.
102013   007792R

Table of Contents

Start with a Seed.....................4

Flower Power.........................12

Apples! 18

Glossary.............................22

Read More...........................23

Internet Sites.......................23

Index................................24

Start with a Seed

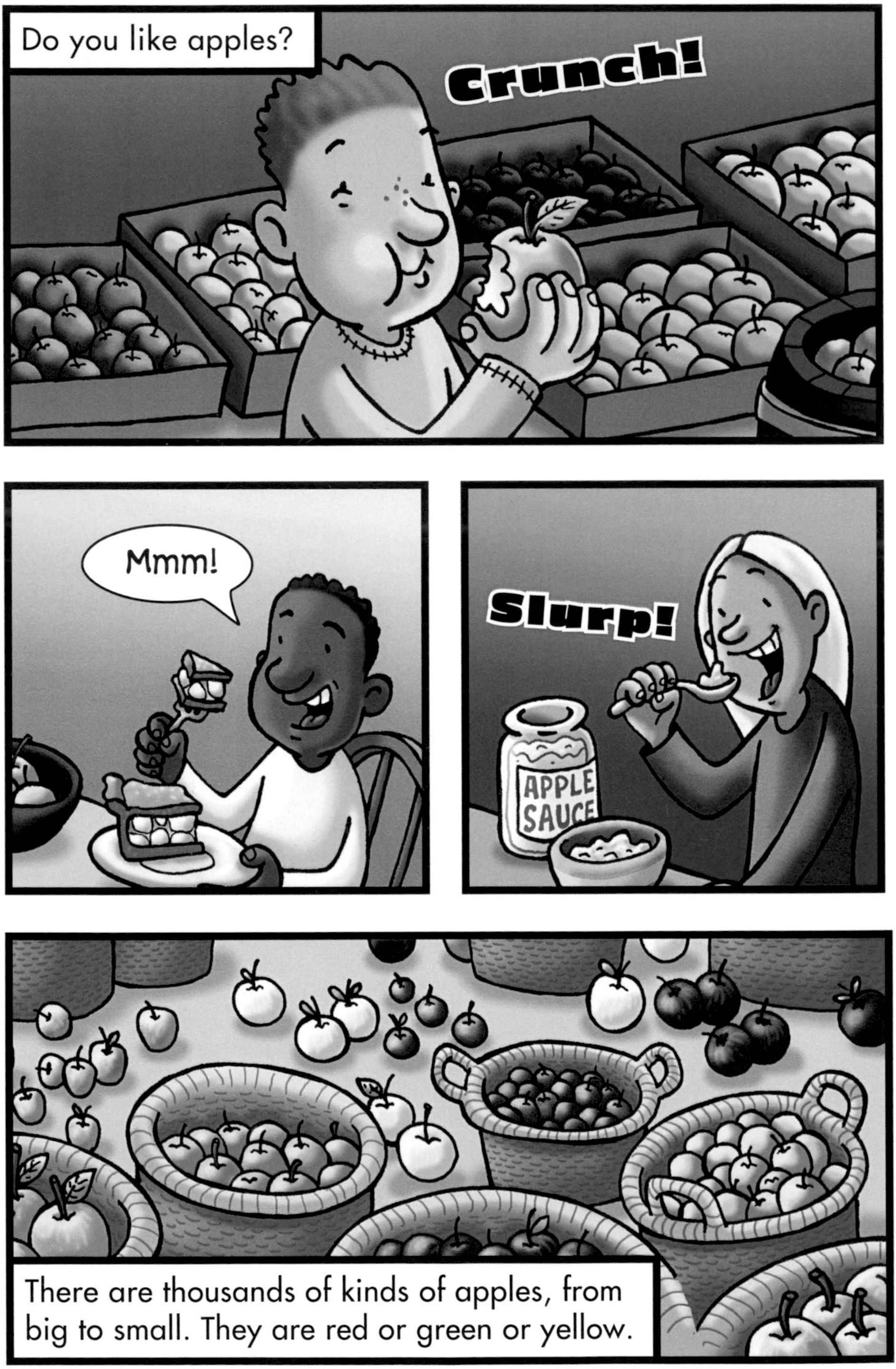
Do you like apples?
Crunch!
Mmm!
Slurp!
APPLE SAUCE
There are thousands of kinds of apples, from big to small. They are red or green or yellow.

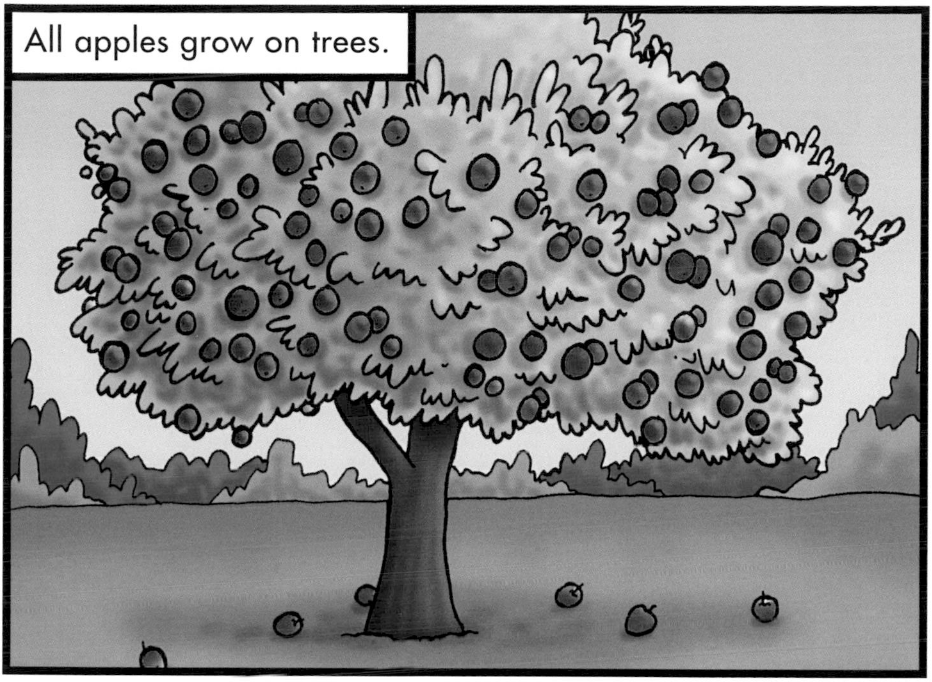
All apples grow on trees.

During its life, an apple tree goes through a series of changes, or cycle.

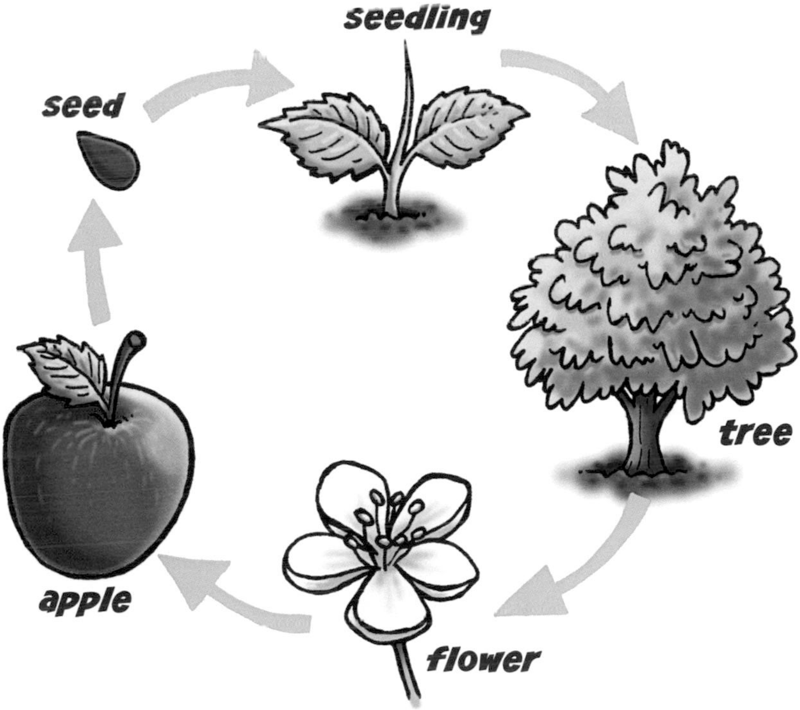
seedling
seed
tree
flower
apple

Apple trees start with a seed in the soil.

Its roots push into the soil. They take in water and minerals.

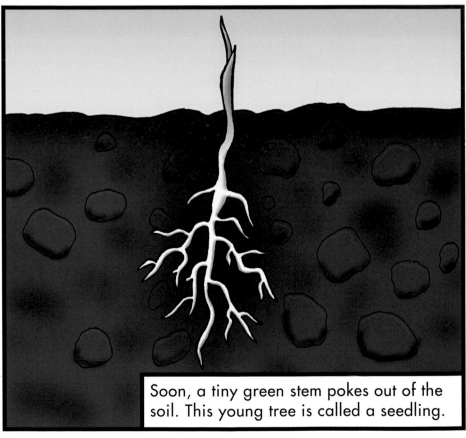

Soon, a tiny green stem pokes out of the soil. This young tree is called a seedling.

As the seedling grows, it sprouts leaves. Chlorophyll in leaves makes them green.

Chlorophyll also helps the tree make food. The leaves take in carbon dioxide (CO_2) gas and energy from sunlight.

Using chlorophyll and water, the tree makes sugar. Sugar gives the seedling energy to grow.

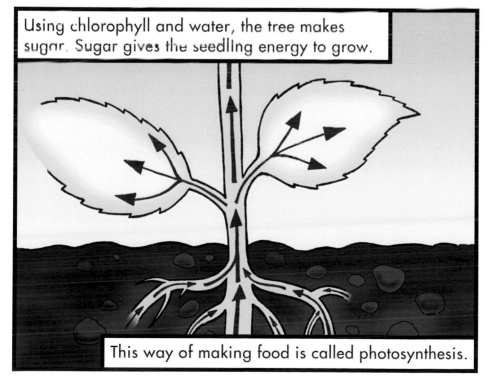

This way of making food is called photosynthesis.

At first, seedlings are tender. Animals may eat them.

Insects may eat the leaves.

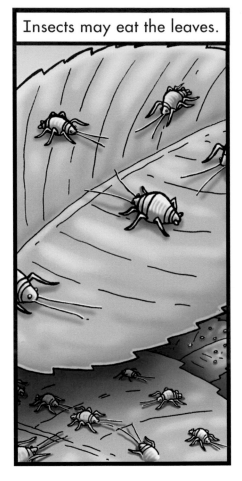

At any time in the life cycle, lack of rain could kill a tree.

Diseases could also kill the apple tree at any age.

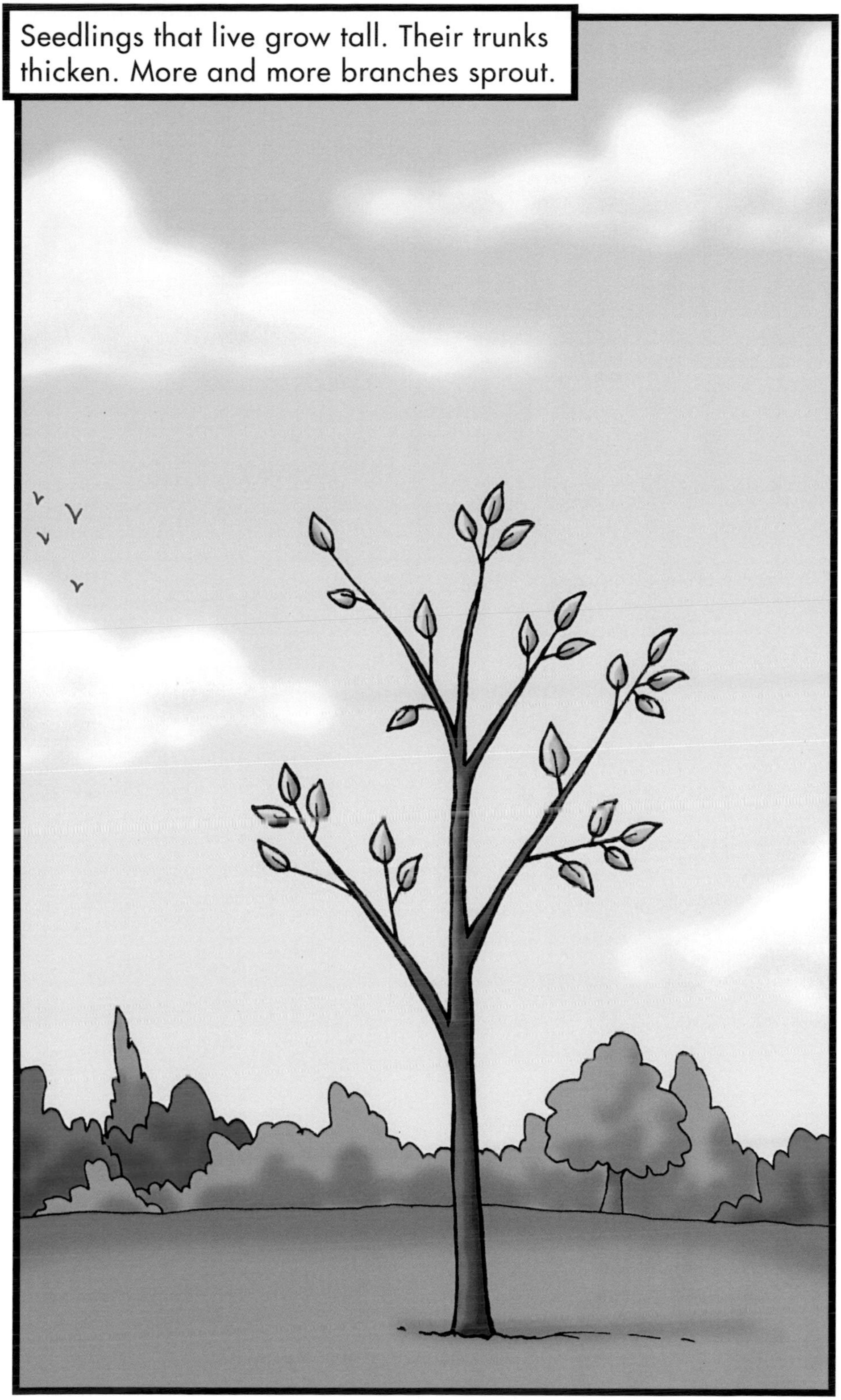
Seedlings that live grow tall. Their trunks thicken. More and more branches sprout.

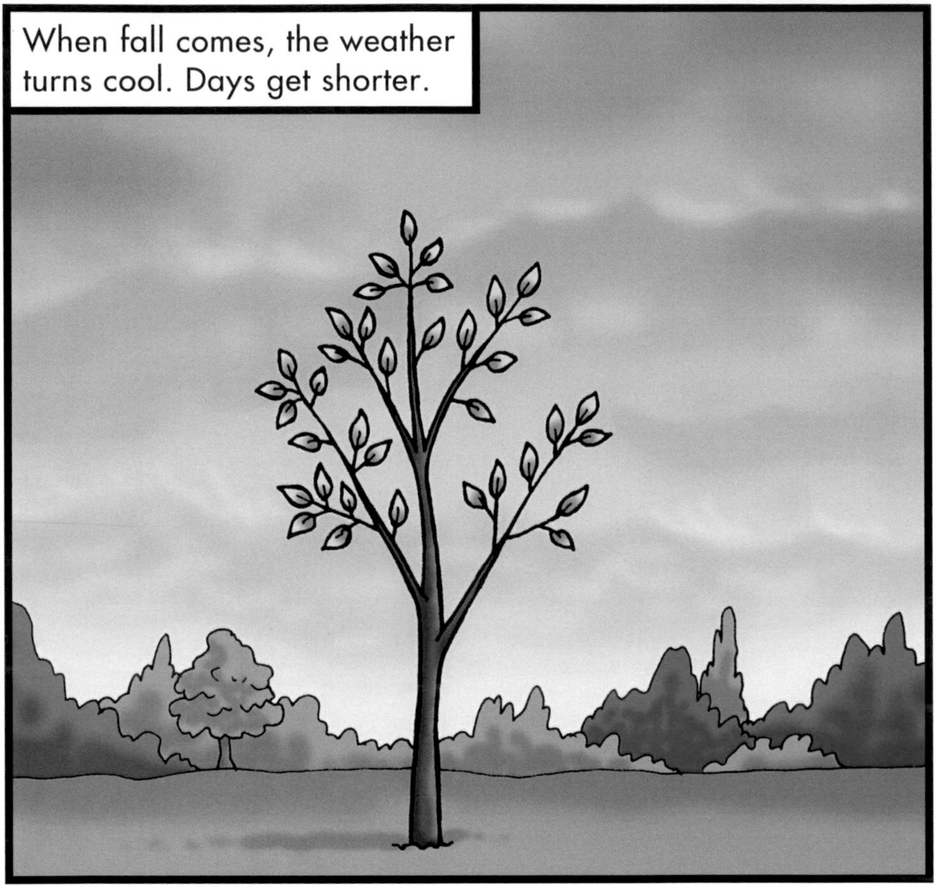
When fall comes, the weather turns cool. Days get shorter.

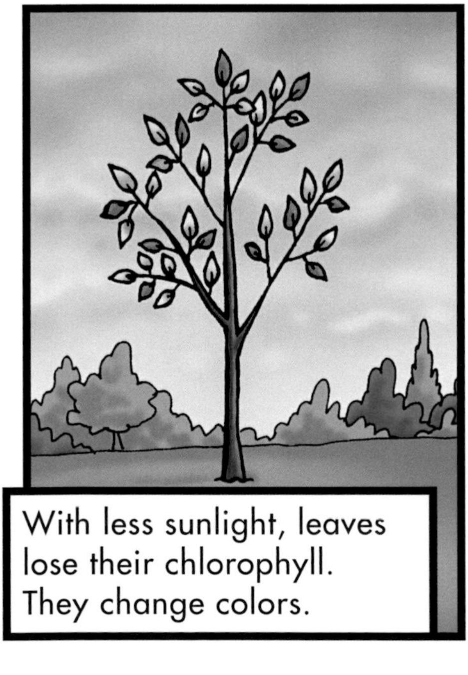
With less sunlight, leaves lose their chlorophyll. They change colors.

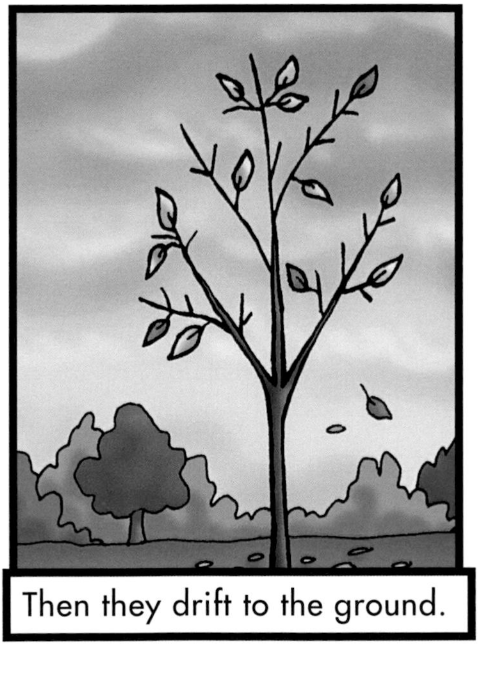
Then they drift to the ground.

Winter comes. The apple tree is bare, but it's still alive. It is dormant.

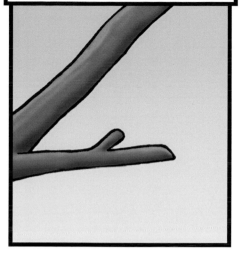

In spring, the little tree gets buds. New leaves open from the buds.

The tree spends four to seven years passing through the seasons, growing bigger and stronger.

Flower Power

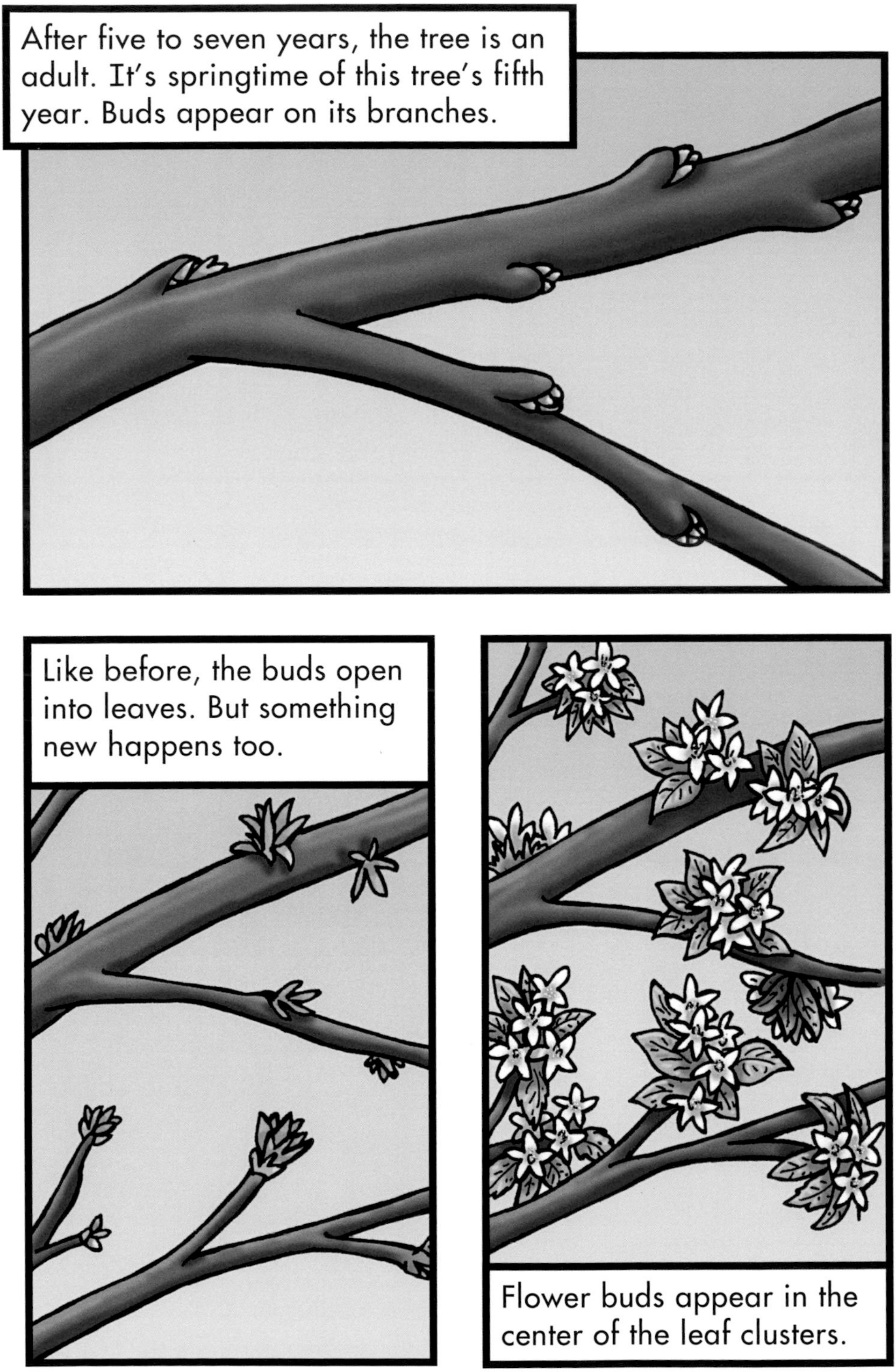
After five to seven years, the tree is an adult. It's springtime of this tree's fifth year. Buds appear on its branches.
Like before, the buds open into leaves. But something new happens too.
Flower buds appear in the center of the leaf clusters.

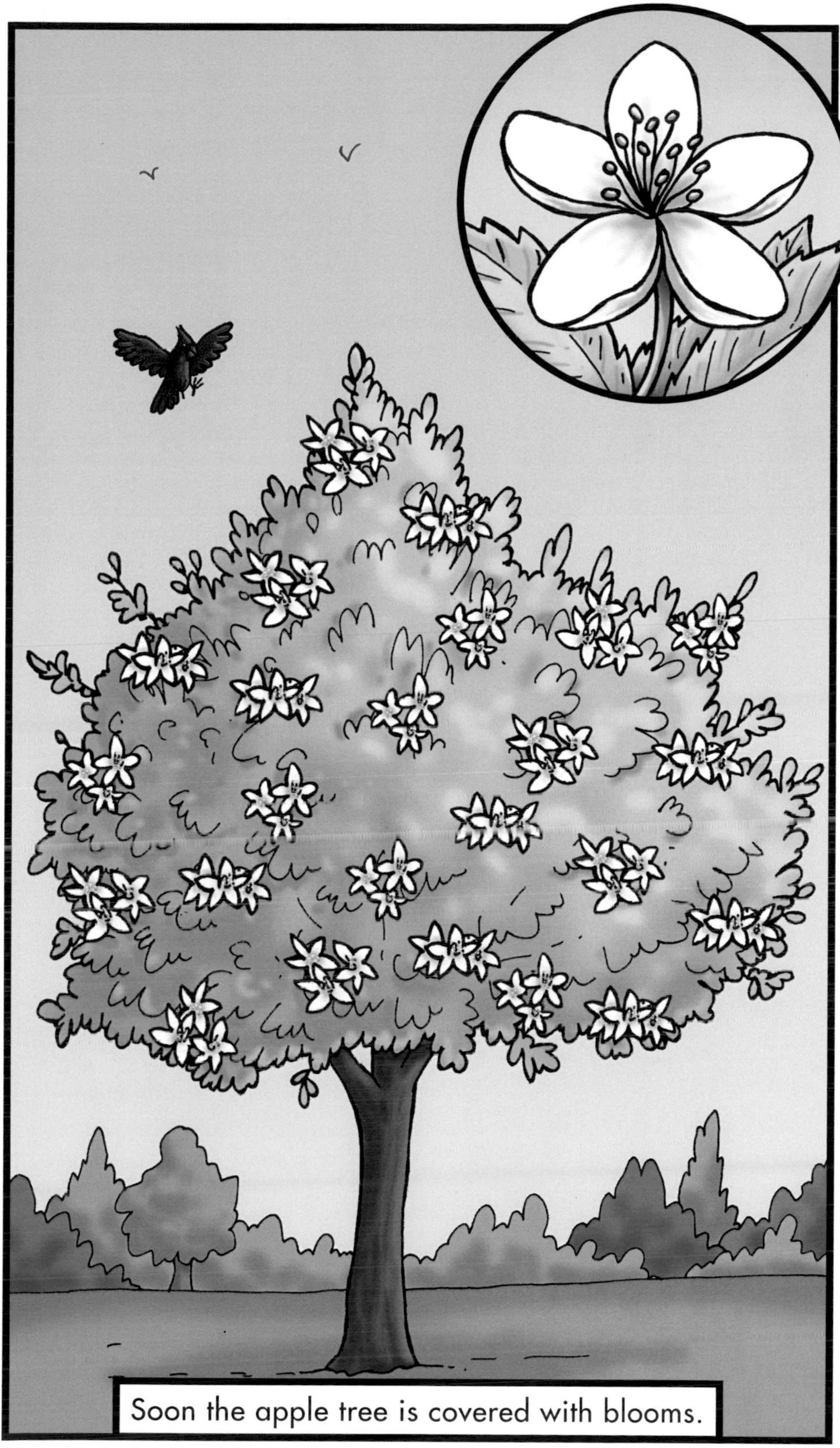

Soon the apple tree is covered with blooms.

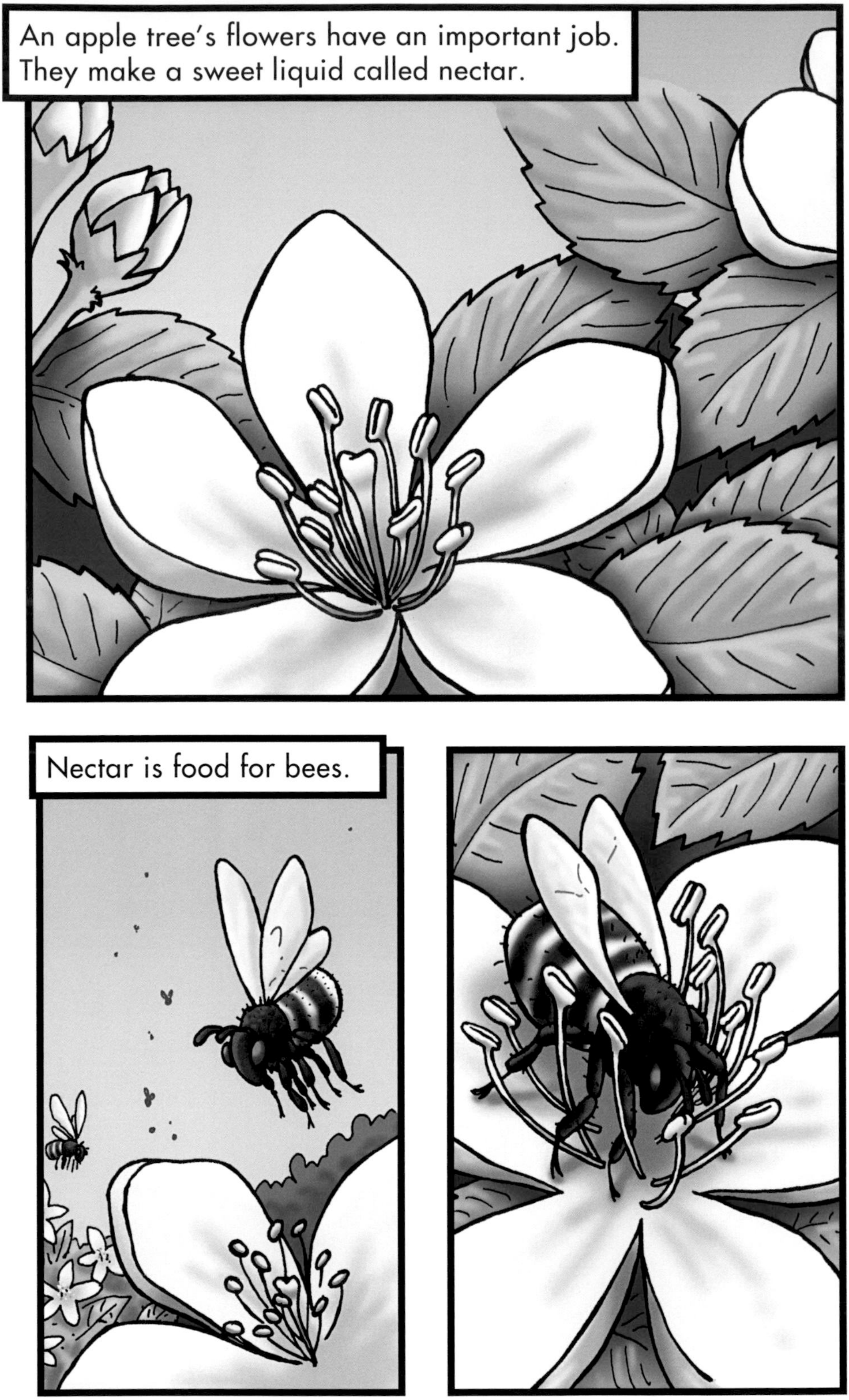
An apple tree's flowers have an important job.
They make a sweet liquid called nectar.
Nectar is food for bees.

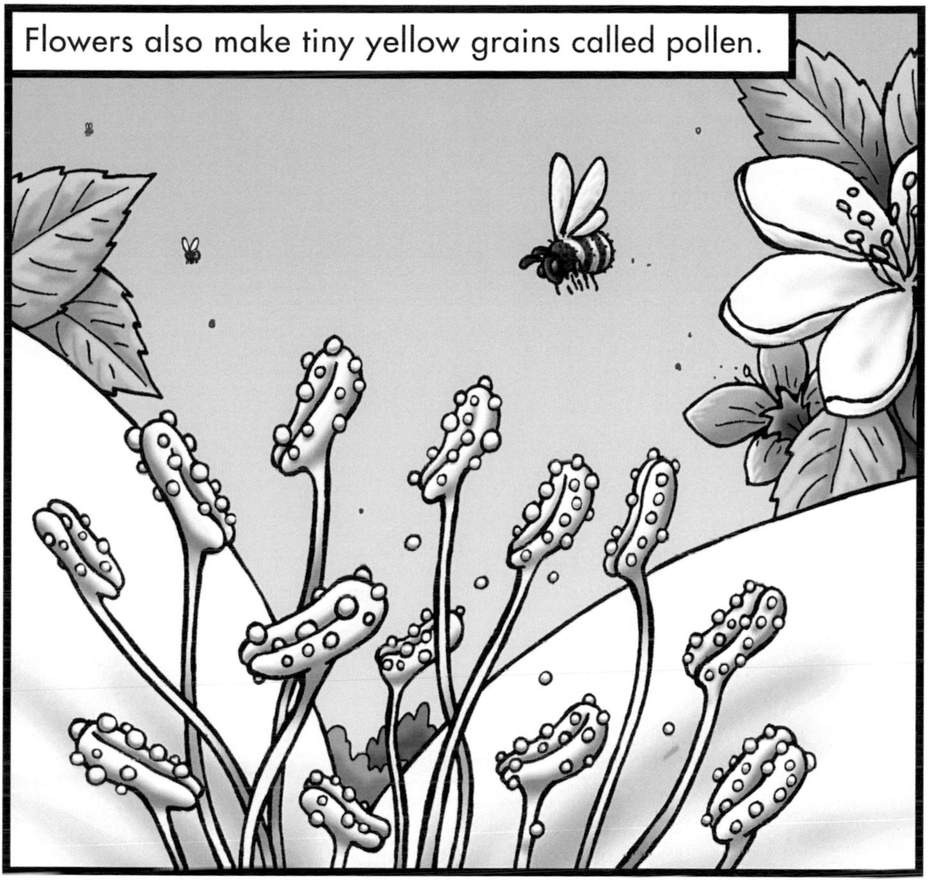
Flowers also make tiny yellow grains called pollen.

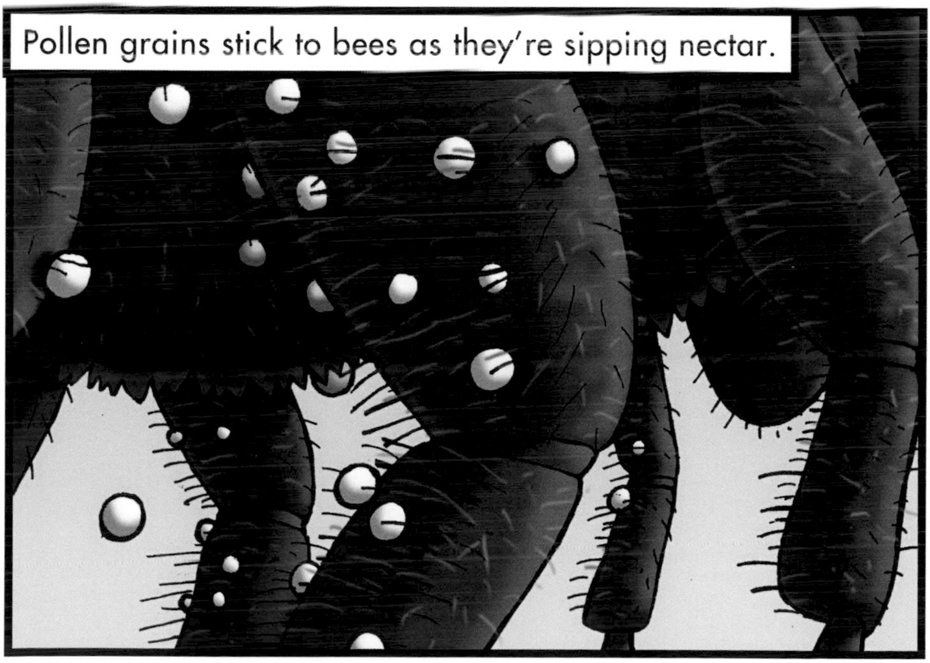
Pollen grains stick to bees as they're sipping nectar.

Bees carry pollen to flowers on other apple trees.

Pollen falls from bees when they land on new flowers.

Pollen makes seeds grow inside the flower.

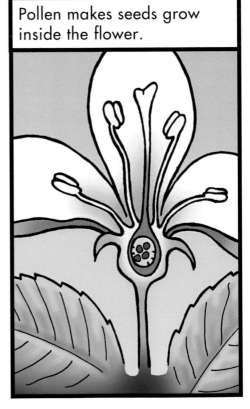

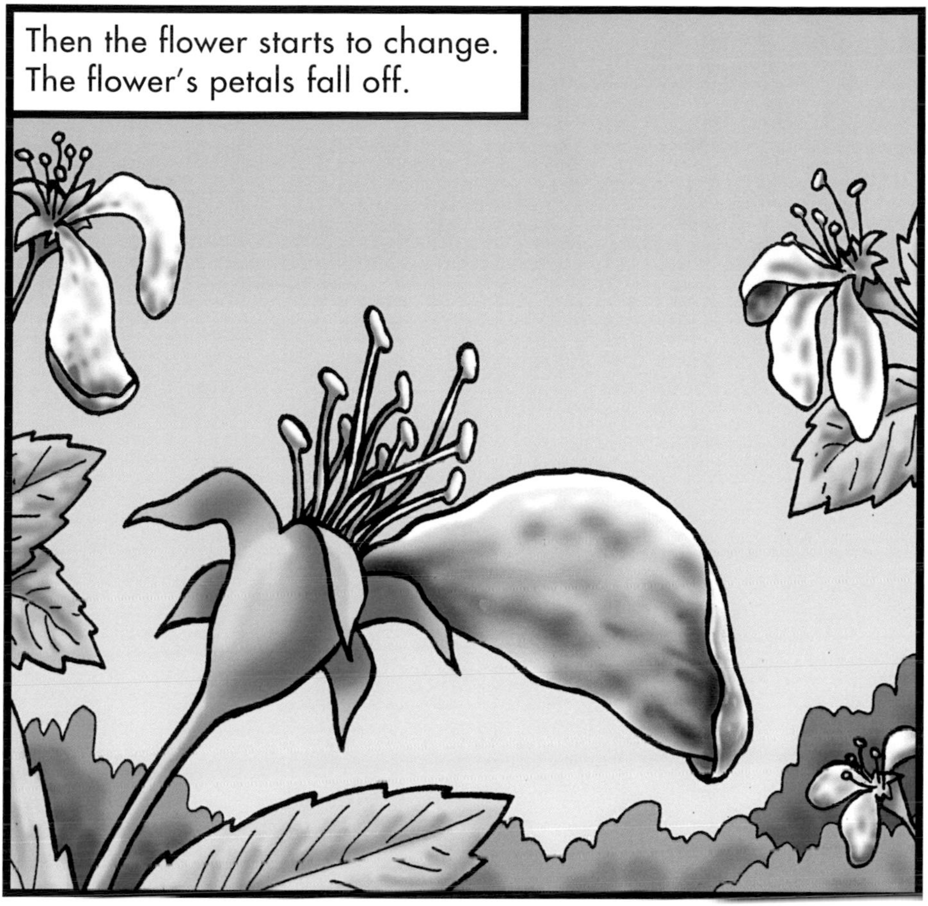
Then the flower starts to change.
The flower's petals fall off.

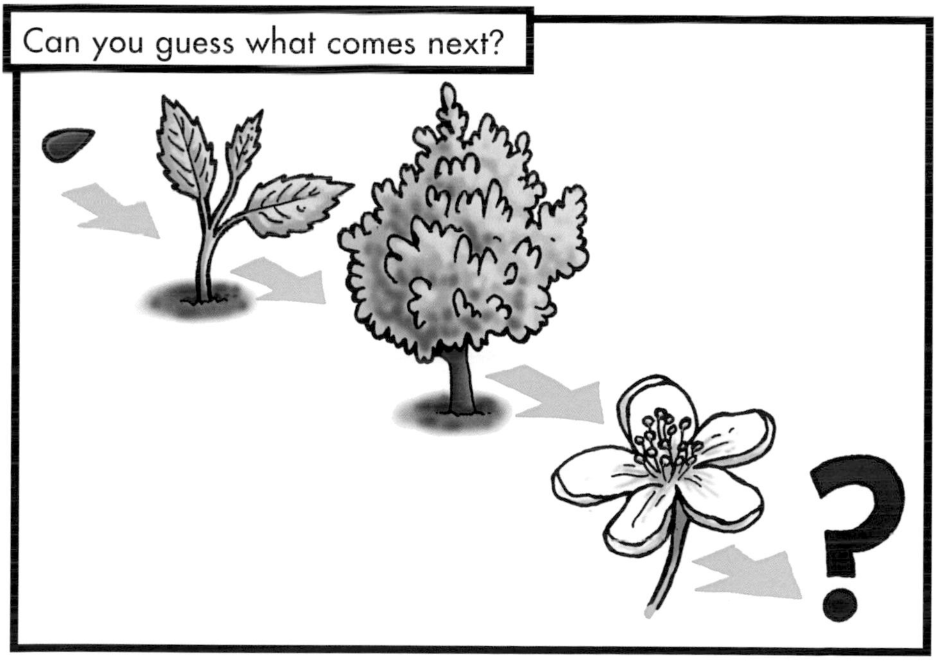
Can you guess what comes next?

Apples!

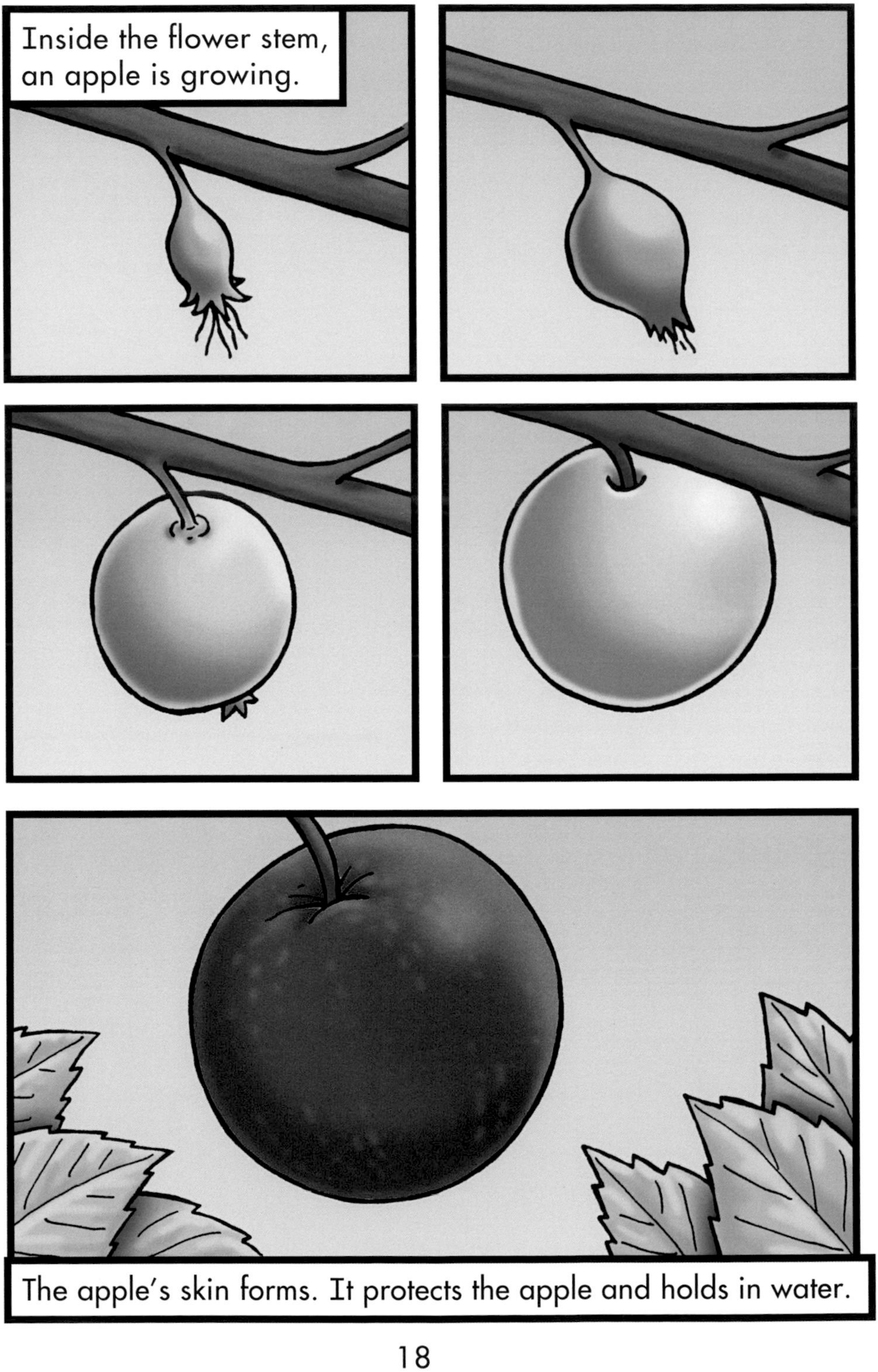
Inside the flower stem, an apple is growing.
The apple's skin forms. It protects the apple and holds in water.

Under the skin is the apple's flesh. Seeds are found in the apple's middle, or core.

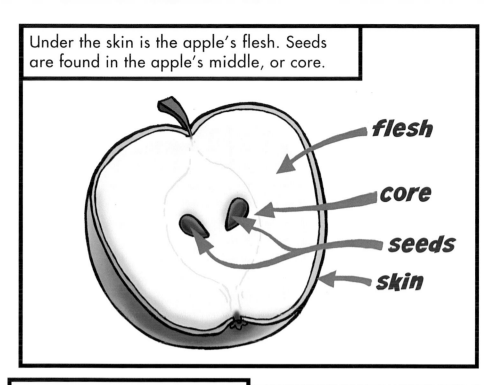

flesh

core

seeds

skin

People aren't the only ones who eat apples. Caterpillars tunnel into apples. They even eat the seeds!

Yuck!

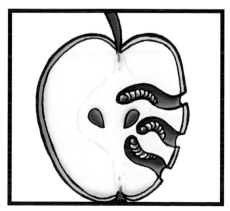

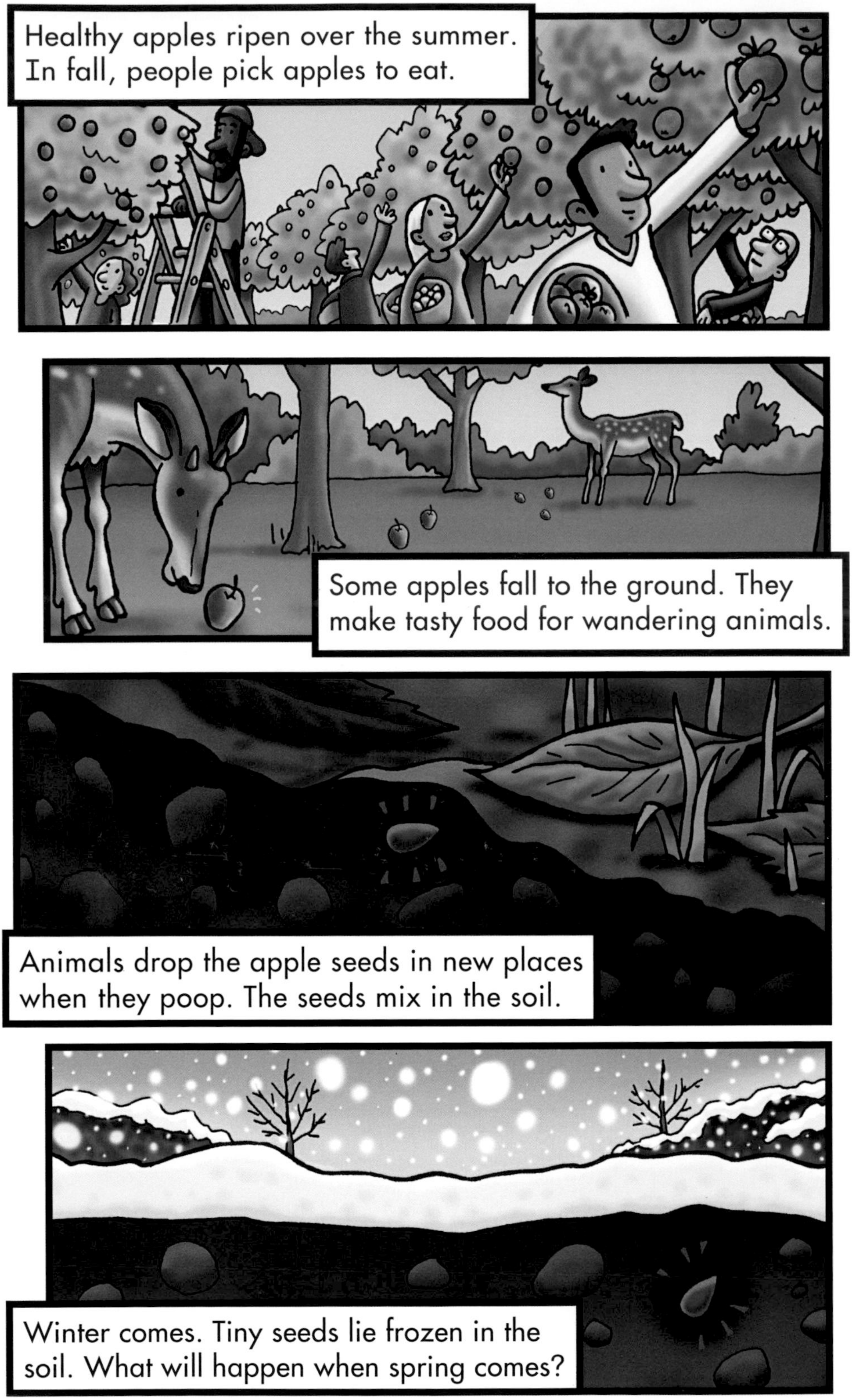
Healthy apples ripen over the summer. In fall, people pick apples to eat.
Some apples fall to the ground. They make tasty food for wandering animals.
Animals drop the apple seeds in new places when they poop. The seeds mix in the soil.
Winter comes. Tiny seeds lie frozen in the soil. What will happen when spring comes?

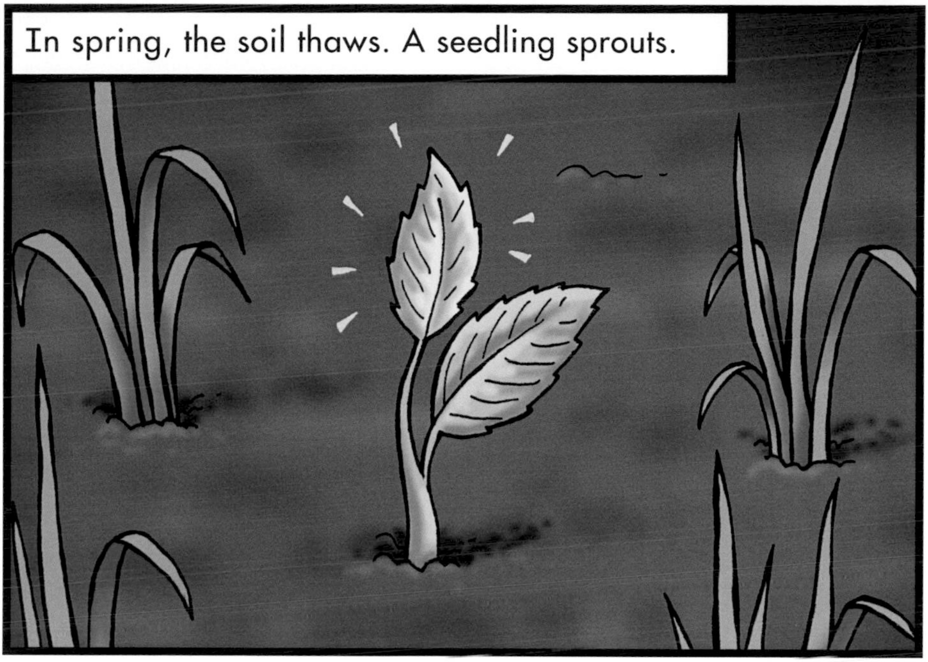
In spring, the soil thaws. A seedling sprouts.

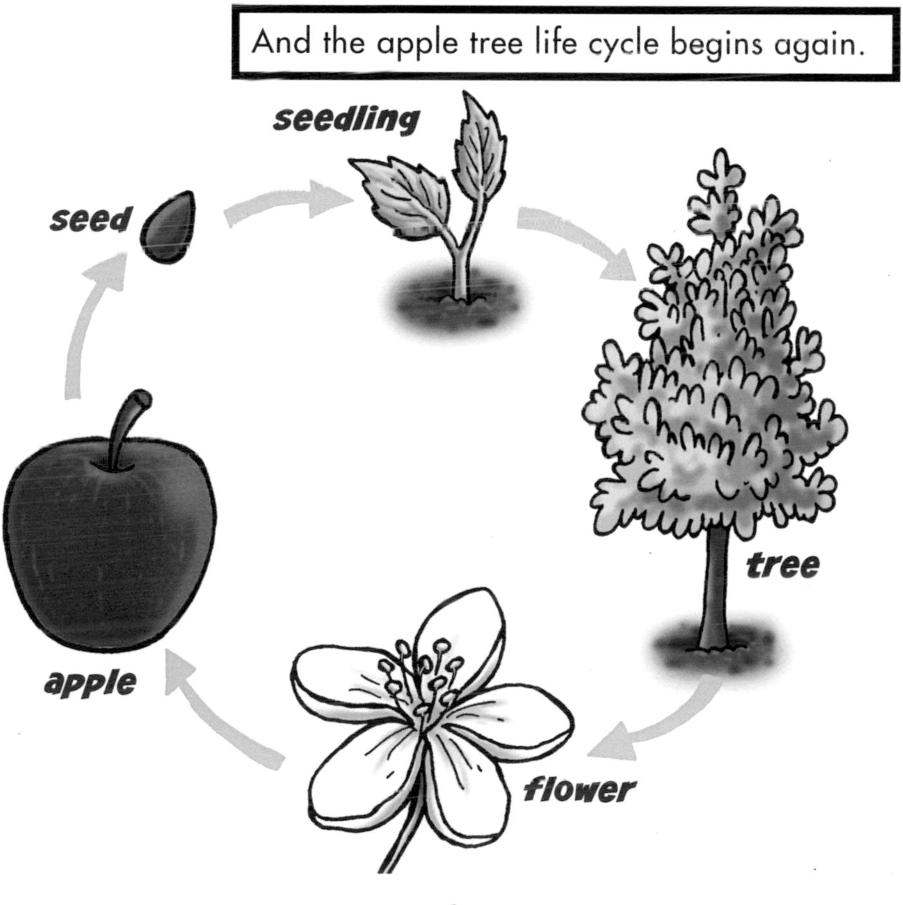
And the apple tree life cycle begins again.
seedling
seed
tree
apple
flower

Glossary

bud—a small shoot on a plant that grows into a leaf or a flower

chlorophyll—the green substance in plants that uses light to make food from carbon dioxide and water

dormant—a state of rest

nectar—a sweet liquid found in many flowers

photosynthesis—the process by which plant cells use energy from the sun to take carbon dioxide, water, and minerals and turn it into food for plants to grow; during this process, trees give off oxygen

pollen—tiny grains that flowers make

root—the part of a plant that grows underground; roots bring water into plants

seedling—a young tree that has grown from a seed

Read More

Royston, Angela. *Life Cycle of an Apple.* Heinemann First Library. Chicago: Heinemann Library, 2009.

Slade, Suzanne. *From Seed to Apple Tree: Following the Life Cycle.* Amazing Science. Life Cycles. Minneapolis: Picture Window Books, 2009.

Thomson, Ruth. *The Life Cycle of an Oak Tree.* Learning about Life Cycles. New York: PowerKids Press, 2009.

Internet Sites

FactHound offers a safe, fun way to find Internet sites related to this book. All of the sites on FactHound have been researched by our staff.

Here's all you do:

Visit www.facthound.com

Type in this code: 9781429653664

Check out projects, games and lots more at
www.capstonekids.com

Index

apples, 4, 5, 18, 20, 21
   colors of, 4
   core of, 19
   flesh of, 19
   sizes of, 4
   skin of, 18, 19
bees, 14–15, 16
branches, 9, 12
buds, 11, 12
carbon dioxide, 7
chlorophyll, 7, 10
dangers to trees, 8
diseases, 8
dormancy, 11
dying, 8
fall (autumn), 10, 20
flowers, 5, 12–13, 14, 15, 16, 17, 18, 21
leaves, 7, 8, 10, 11, 12
minerals, 6
nectar, 14, 15

photosynthesis, 7
pollen, 15, 16
ripening, 20
roots, 6
seedlings, 5, 6–7, 8–9, 21
seeds, 5, 6, 16, 19, 20, 21
soil, 6, 20
spring, 11, 12, 20–21
sunlight, 7, 10
trunks, 9
water, 6, 7, 18
winter, 11, 20

TITLES IN THIS SET:

EGGS, LEGS, WINGS
A Butterfly Life Cycle

HIDE and SEEK MOON
The Moon Phases

SEED, SPROUT, FRUIT
An Apple Tree Life Cycle

WATER GOES ROUND
The Water Cycle